LIFE ISN'T FAIR

Most Perigee Books are available at special quantity discounts for bulk purchases for sales promotions, premiums, fund-raising or educational use. Special books, or book excerpts, can also be created to fit specific needs.

For details, write: Special Markets, The Berkley Publishing Group, 200 Madison Avenue, New York, New York 10016.

LIFE ISN'T FAIR

300 YEARS OF ADVICE FROM HISTORY'S MOST MEMORABLE COMMENCEMENTS

Harold Hill

A Perigee Book

A Perigee Book
Published by The Berkley Publishing Group
200 Madison Avenue
New York, NY 10016

Copyright © 1997 by David Colbert
Book design by Casey Hampton
Cover design by Dale Fiorello.

First edition: May 1997

Published simultaneously in Canada

The Putnam Berkley World Wide Web site address is
http://www.berkley.com

Library of Congress Cataloging-in-Publication Data

Life isn't fair : 300 years of advice form history's most memorable
    commencements / [compiled by] Harold Hill.—1st ed.
        p.   cm.
    "A Perigee book."
    ISBN 0-399-52301-4
    1. Life—Quotations, maxims, etc. 2. Conduct of life—Quotations,
maxims, etc. 3. Baccalaureate addresses. I. Hill, Harold, 1963–.
II. Title: Life is not fair.
PN6084.L53L54   1997
081—DC20   96-36560
                                                                     CIP

Printed in the United States of America

10 9 8 7 6 5 4 3 2 1

For Lynda S. Duckworth,
who prevented my expulsion,
and my parents,
who helped type the applications.

I wish you much weirdness in your lives.

—Gary Larson, cartoonist,
creator of "The Far Side"
Washington State University, 1990

Ordinarily a speaker at a commencement is awarded an honorary degree just before he speaks. In some cases, however, he is instead given an honorarium just after he speaks. Either one makes him feel important, and this is vital, for he cannot play his role properly unless he is well aware that what he says is the important feature of the day. . . . He must behave as if the whole success or failure of the ceremony depends upon him. He must have a ringing message, and he must deliver it loudly, in considerable detail, and with gestures.

—Barnaby C. Keeney,
president of the university,
Brown University, 1964

Contents

Contents

Acknowledgments

Thanks to Desa Philadelphia, Sharon Cohen, and Karen Scofield for their excellent research.

Thanks also to the New York Public Library and the Television News Archive at Vanderbilt University.

I am also grateful for the expertise of everyone at Putnam/Perigee, including John Duff, Jennifer Kantor Wood, and Mih-Ho Cha.

And, as always, I am indebted to my parents, my sisters Jan and Melanie, and to many friends, including Ursula Bollini, Marc de La Bruyère, Ani Chamichian, Christine Dowson, Lisa Feuer, Amy Hertz, Daniel Huang, Henry Huang, Lyuba Konopasek, Matthew Kronby, Miles Kronby, Garrett Loubé, Alison Macondray, Theresa Menders, Bonnie Nadell, Peter Pfau, Carolyn Pittis, Bob Rochelle, Marcia Rodgers, Leslie Rossman, Stacy Schiff, Ben Shykind, Kim Starr, Frank Takao and Wanda Takao.

INTRODUCTION

In a darkened vault in Columbia University's rare book library, one of the first books printed in America is kept safe from the destructive effects of the elements. Several generations of caretakers have preserved it well over more than 300 years.

Written by an author known only as "R.L.," the book is also noteworthy for its text, although whether it deserves credit or blame for its role is largely a matter of taste. Like ancient cave drawings that presage the styles of Picasso and Kandinsky, Columbia's relic establishes an early date for the ignoble American genre "Advice, How-to and Miscellaneous." It is titled *Letter of Advice to a Young Gentleman upon Leaving the University Concerning his Behaviour and Conversation in the World.* It is full of amusing and insightful advice that still rings true, such as, "Let not the Lapses or ridiculous Accidents or Behaviours of Men in Drink or in Love be taken notice of after . . . for no man loves to have his folly remembered."

In 1696, when it was published, the market for the book could not have been large. William and Mary was only two years old; Harvard was the only American college minting graduates. Yet now, with millions of new graduates leaving high schools and colleges each year, the desire to give and receive life lessons remains as strong as ever.

Some of the advice is different now. Until this century, most commencement speeches were sermons. Today's commencements are more likely to feature a movie star than a minister. But while the religious messages are less frequent, the other favorite subjects—challenges, responsibilities, parents, character, and the like—remain the same.

Here, then, is three hundred years of advice and wisecracks, brickbats and bouquets. Now please return the gown.

—Harold Hill

Now the only thing standing between you and a degree is, well, me.
And eighteen minutes.

—S. FREDERICK STARR, AUTHOR
COLLEGE OF WOOSTER, 1995

THE REAL WORLD

Young ladies and gentlemen, I am told that you are going out in the world today. Don't.

—BOB HOPE, COMEDIAN
UNIVERSITY OF CALIFORNIA, LOS ANGELES, 1965

I shall not tell you that you are the hope of the world. I was told that on the occasion of three commencements: high school, college, and graduate school. Well, look at the world!

—REV. JAMES MCLEOD, CHAPLAIN,
NORTHWESTERN UNIVERSITY
MIDDLEBURY COLLEGE, 1952

People will frighten you about a graduation...because they use words you don't hear often... "And we wish you Godspeed." It is a warning, "Godspeed." It means you are no longer welcome here at these prices.

—BILL COSBY, COMEDIAN
SOUTHERN METHODIST UNIVERSITY, 1995

In the real world, dreams do not come equipped with the magic wands of Cinderella stories.

—ABELARDO L. VALDEZ, U.S. AMBASSADOR
TEXAS A&M UNIVERSITY, 1994

My job is to bore you and let the hardness of your seat and the warmth of your robe prepare you for what is to come.

—Dr. William H. McNeill,
University of Chicago historian
Bard College, 1984

Life is rough for everyone.... Life isn't always fair. Whatever it is that hits the fan, it's never evenly distributed—some always tend to get more of it than others.

—Ann Landers, columnist
Southwestern Adventist College, 1987

A substantial part of what lies ahead of you is going to be claimed by boredom. The reason I'd like to talk to you about it today, on this lofty occasion, is that I believe no liberal arts college prepares you for that eventuality.... You'll be bored with your work, your friends, your spouses, your lovers, the view from your window, the furniture or wallpaper in your room, your thoughts, yourselves. Accordingly, you'll try to devise ways of escape ... you may take up changing your job, residence, company, country, climate; you may take up promiscuity, alcohol, travel, cooking lessons, drugs, psychoanalysis....

[But] if it takes will-paralyzing boredom to bring your insignificance home, then hail the boredom. You are insignificant because you are finite.... And the more finite a thing is, the more it is charged with life, emotions, joy, fears, compassion.

—JOSEPH BRODSKY, AUTHOR
DARTMOUTH COLLEGE, 1995

Life is long. You'll have lots of opportunities, lots of different things to do, and you don't have to do them all at once. You can, you just don't sleep very much. I've never played any sports so that saves a lot of time.

—COKIE ROBERTS, JOURNALIST
BRYN MAWR COLLEGE, 1990

There are some really terrible times ahead. Everyone has them. But life, all in all, can be spectacularly good. If this were not so, none of us my age and older would be so desperately trying to fend off our impending demise.

—ANDY ROONEY,
CBS COMMENTATOR (AT HIS ALMA MATER)
COLGATE UNIVERSITY, 1996

In all things be willing to listen to people around you. None of us is really smart enough to go it alone.

—JOHN L. CLENDENIN,
CHAIRMAN AND CEO OF BELLSOUTH CORP.
GEORGIA STATE UNIVERSITY, 1991

Get out there, work hard, and thank God we're living in a country where the sky's the limit, the stores are open late, and you can shop in bed thanks to television.

—JOAN RIVERS, COMEDIAN
UNIVERSITY OF PENNSYLVANIA, 1989

What everybody says is absolutely true. These are, or these were, the halcyon days. Real life is actually a lot more like high school. The common denominator prevails. Excellence is not always recognized or rewarded. What we watch on our screens, whom we elect, are determined to a large extent by public polls. Looks count. A lot. And unlike the best of the college experience, when ideas and solutions somehow seem attainable if you just get up early, stay up late, try hard enough, and find the right source or method, things on the outside sometimes seem vast and impossible, and *settling*, resigning oneself, or hiding and hunkering down becomes the best way of getting along. . . .

That choice, between the devil and the dream, comes up every day in little disguises. I'm sure it comes up in every field of endeavor and every life. My advice is to look the dilemma in the face and decide what you can live with. If you can live with the devil, Vassar hasn't sunk her teeth into your leg the way she did mine.

—MERYL STREEP, ACTRESS
VASSAR COLLEGE, 1985

Men are sluggish, and gravitate towards sensuality; they fall into habits and routine, and run in ruts; they carry the grain on one side of the horse, and a stone on the other, because their fathers did.... There is nothing that men have been so reluctant to do as to think. They would go on pilgrimages, hang on hooks, accept dogmas, bow down to power, but they have been slow to put forth their powers in an earnest effort after comprehension and enlargement.

—Mark Hopkins, president of the college
Williams College, 1863

The world is good for what it was intended to be; but an inn is not a home.... If the world shall disappoint you, it will be your own fault.

—Mark Hopkins, president of the college
Williams College, 1872

People always get what they want. But there is a price for everything. Failures are either those who do not know what they want or are not prepared to pay the price asked them. The price varies from individual to individual. Some get things at bargain-sale prices, others only at famine prices. But it is no use grumbling. Whatever price you are asked, you must pay.

—W. H. AUDEN, POET
SMITH COLLEGE, 1940

[This is] not a world governed by ethics or by men who know history. . . . It is a world run by old men.

—EDWARD R. MURROW, JOURNALIST
SMITH COLLEGE, 1947

We are merely endeavoring to say that by virtue of her unusual training and equipment the college graduate will find herself at first somewhat out of touch with the rest of mankind.

—MARION LE ROY BURTON, PRESIDENT OF THE COLLEGE
SMITH COLLEGE, 1914

The world is more than a game of cards. History is more than a record of gambling operations.

—ARTHUR TWINING HADLEY,
PRESIDENT OF THE UNIVERSITY
YALE UNIVERSITY, 1903

Think what a better world it would be if we all, the whole world, had cookies and milk about three o'clock every afternoon and then lay down on our blankets for a nap.

—BARBARA JORDAN, CONGRESSPERSON
MIDDLEBURY COLLEGE, 1987

Every generation has the obligation to free men's minds for a look at new worlds, to look out from a higher plateau than the last generation. When I circled the moon and looked back at the Earth, my outlook on life and my viewpoint of Earth changed. By holding up my thumb at arm's length, I could completely blot out our planet. I suddenly realized how insignificant we are.

—CAPT. JAMES LOVELL, ASTRONAUT
WESTERN MONTANA COLLEGE, 1983

You people are not prepared. You are well educated and you look cute, but that's not going to cut it.

—BILL COSBY, COMEDIAN
UNIVERSITY OF MARYLAND, 1992

CHALLENGES

Today's challenge is mostly to avoid embarrassing Madeline.

—Mario Cuomo, Governor of New York
State University of New York at Albany, 1986
(Madeline Cuomo was in the graduating class.)

What I want to tell you today is not to move into that world where you're alone with yourself and your mantra and your fitness program or whatever it is that you might use to try to control the world by closing it out. I want to tell you to just live in the mess. Throw yourself out into the convulsions of the world. I'm not telling you to make the world better because I don't believe progress is necessarily part of the package. I'm just telling you to live in it, to look at it, to witness it. Try and get it. Take chances, make your own work, take pride in it. Seize the moment.

—Joan Didion, author
Bard College, 1987

You are responsible for the world that you live in. It is not government's responsibility. It is not your school's or your social club's or your church's or your neighbor's or your fellow citizen's. It is yours, utterly and singularly yours.

—AUGUST WILSON, PLAYWRIGHT
HAMLINE UNIVERSITY, 1990

When you go out into this world, remember: compassion, compassion, compassion.

—BETTY WILLIAMS, WINNER OF THE 1977 NOBEL PEACE PRIZE
NORTH HARRIS MONTGOMERY COMMUNITY COLLEGE
DISTRICT, 1994

I have observed a number of superficially contented men and women . . . and I maintain they are dangerous. Personally, I am glad to say there are a lot of things today with which I am not contented. . . . I am not contented with the road system in Newbury . . . nor do I like the control of mosquitoes. . . . I am not contented with the Boston & Maine Railroad . . . nor do I like the way poison ivy keeps growing near my house. I am not contented either with the United Nations or with the general situation in Europe. . . . I am not contented with myself . . . with the development of my character . . . and with my literary career. . . . At any rate, there seems to me very little ground for general contentment . . . and I must repeat . . . I fear the contented man. I fear him because there is no progress unless there is discontent. Without it I believe there can be no inner peace of mind.

—JOHN P. MARQUAND, NOVELIST
GOVERNOR DUMMER ACADEMY, 1949

If America is to remain a first-class nation she can no longer have second-class citizens.

—Dr. Martin Luther King, Jr., civil rights leader
Lincoln University, 1961

We are not free by simply stating that we are free, no matter how often or how eloquently we say it.

—J. Martin Klotsche, president of the college
Milwaukee State Teachers College, 1952

Adapt quickly to the drudgery of everyday life and put your knowledge to good work.

—WILLIAM HOWARD TAFT, U.S. PRESIDENT
BRYN MAWR COLLEGE, 1910

A few years ago we were greatly concerned about the "Ugly American." Today we must act to prevent an Ugly America.

—LYNDON B. JOHNSON, U.S. PRESIDENT
UNIVERSITY OF MICHIGAN, 1964

Open yourselves to the breathtaking changes...that have already rendered obsolete much of what you have learned in class.

...I ask you not to be dazzled by the kaleidoscope of human life to believe that people who are different than you have different needs and aspirations.

—JOHN MARBURGER, PRESIDENT OF THE UNIVERSITY
SUNY STONY BROOK, 1990

There has always been change, there always will be change.... It's to our young people that I look for the new ideas. No computer is ever going to ask a new, reasonable question. It takes trained people to do that. And if we're going to move toward those things we'd like to have, we must have the young to ask the new, reasonable questions. A ship in port is safe: but that is not what ships are built for.

—GRACE HORN, REAR ADMIRAL (RETIRED) U.S. NAVY,
COMPUTER PIONEER
TRINITY COLLEGE, 1987

The only thing worth living for is the lifting up of our fellow men.

—BOOKER T. WASHINGTON, PRESIDENT OF THE COLLEGE
TUSKEGEE INSTITUTE, 1891

The great problem confronting us today is that we have allowed the means by which we live to outdistance the ends for which we live. We have allowed our civilization to outrun our culture, and so we are in the danger now of ending up with guided missiles in the hands of misguided men.

—DR. MARTIN LUTHER KING, JR., CIVIL RIGHTS LEADER
LINCOLN UNIVERSITY, 1961

The young black captain just back from Vietnam thirty years ago who couldn't get a hamburger at a Georgia restaurant unless he went to the back window has become chairman of the Joint Chiefs of Staff. . . . All of us have to remember the brave people who went before and upon whose backs we climbed. . . . As we climbed on the backs of others, so must we allow our backs to be used for others to go even higher than we have.

—General Colin Powell,
Chairman, Joint Chiefs of Staff
Fisk University, 1992

You're here because you were given a student loan. Because somebody else paid his off. Pay yours off. Start the next step by being honest.

—BILL COSBY, COMEDIAN
UNIVERSITY OF CONNECTICUT, 1996

If the era of big government is over, then the era of big citizens must begin. If we're not going to have government programs to create a Great Society, we'd better have Great Citizens who can act on the problems which are festering and mounting in our midst.

—HARRIS WOFFORD, FORMER U.S. SENATOR
FAIRFIELD UNIVERSITY, 1996

If you ever think you're too small to be effective, you've never been in bed with a mosquito.

—Anita Roddick, founder of The Body Shop
Trinity College of Vermont, 1996

This must be an era when the soul catches up with the brain, when soul directs science, when motives master machines, when how men feel becomes as important as what men know.

—Rev. Louis Hadley Evans, educator
University of Kansas, 1952

I graduated with a class committed to open love, open thinking, open doors, open everything.... Twenty-two years later, the people of my class are getting cash out of a machine, dinner out of a clown's mouth, and it isn't even possible to get a human being on the phone at the phone company.... If you want something to change, you personally have to do something different.... Defy your own group. Rebel against yourself. Knock down your walls and get out of your way.

—CATHY GUISEWITE,
CARTOONIST AND CREATOR OF "CATHY"
UNIVERSITY OF MICHIGAN, 1994

Remember, if there's no struggle, there is no progress.

—RACHEL ROBINSON (WIFE OF JACKIE ROBINSON,
FOUNDER OF THE JACKIE ROBINSON FOUNDATION)
NEW YORK UNIVERSITY, 1996

Government may build a hospital. But we must visit the sick and comfort the dying. Government must build schools—good schools—but parents are the ultimate teachers. Government can build libraries and parks and gyms, but we must encourage the children of broken homes and mean streets to read and play and grow and not join gangs or do drugs.

—FEDERICO PEÑA, SECRETARY OF TRANSPORTATION
UNIVERSITY OF TEXAS AT AUSTIN, 1994

Too often we consider race as something only blacks have, sex orientation as something only gays have, gender as something only women have. If we don't fall into any of these categories, then we don't have to worry.... In the twenty-first century the problem is ethnic identity as forty-eight countries are ravaged by ethnic violence. Who would have thought twenty years ago when you mentioned ethnic violence in Georgia in 1995, you'd be talking about the Soviet Union rather than the United States?... The stronger a sense you nurture of the contingent nature of all such identities, the less likely you will be harmed by them, or in their name inflict harm on others.

—HENRY LOUIS GATES, JR., PROFESSOR AND AUTHOR
EMORY UNIVERSITY, 1995

All of us need to lower our voices. All of us need to look at our common purposes.

—DONNA SHALALA,
U.S. SECRETARY OF HEALTH AND HUMAN SERVICES
CITY UNIVERSITY OF NEW YORK GRADUATE CENTER, 1995

It is not enough to get things done; they must be done right.... To make our work count in the final result, it must have purpose as well as efficiency.

—ARTHUR TWINING HADLEY,
PRESIDENT OF THE UNIVERSITY
YALE UNIVERSITY, 1906

Whether or not you reach your goals in life depends entirely on how well you prepare for them and how badly you want them.

—Ronald McNair, astronaut
Howard University, 1983

Risk is a turn-on.

—Frances Lear, magazine publisher
Long Island University (Southhampton campus), 1990

It is you, and only you, who determine who you will be and what you will do for the rest of your lives. . . . Wellesley has uniquely qualified you to create your own images without the blinders of past stereotypes. . . . No goal should be beyond your reach.

No wonder, then, that any disturbance of the stereotypes seems like an attack upon the foundations of the universe. It *is* an attack on the foundations of our universe. . . . If we do not do what is expected of us, it challenges others and their secure and standardized view of the world.

—JILL WINE-VOLNER, SECRETARY, DEPARTMENT OF JUSTICE;
GENERAL COUNSEL, DEPARTMENT OF THE ARMY
WELLESLEY COLLEGE, 1978

The world needs specialists and highly trained people with advanced degrees, no question about it. But the world also needs diversity and versatility. It needs people who know as much about our value system as they do about our solar system.

—ROGER B. SMITH, CHAIRMAN, GENERAL MOTORS CORPORATION
ALBION COLLEGE, 1982

In the last few years, we have witnessed a celebration, even a sanctification, of self-concern. A person's highest duty, it holds, is to his own income. This attitude is a powerful attack on the least fortunate of our citizens.... Perhaps the disadvantaged are now too few in the United States to make a revolution. But they could make life uncomfortable for all.

—JOHN KENNETH GALBRAITH, ECONOMIST
HAVERFORD COLLEGE, 1980

Do not follow where the path may lead, go instead where there is no path and leave a trail.

—Bob Rivera and Peter Yates, janitors
Kingswood Regional High, 1991

(Kingswood's two custodians, Bob Rivera and Peter Yates, were chosen by unanimous vote of the 115 graduating seniors to deliver the commencement address. They received a standing ovation for their speech. An hour later, they were taking apart the stage and picking up garbage. "We're probably the only commencement speakers in history," said Rivera, "who've had to clean up after themselves.")

Look outward.... Perhaps previous ages suffered from a lack of self-examination. The Age of Oprah does not. One of the defining features of modernity is self-consciousness: psychological self-consciousness as popularized by Freud; historical self-consciousness as introduced by Hegel and Marx; literary self-consciousness as practiced in the interior, self-referential, self-absorbed world of modern fiction.

The reigning cliché of the day is that in order to love others one must first learn to love oneself. This formulation—love thyself, then thy neighbor—is a license for unremitting self-indulgence, because the quest for self-love is endless. By the time you have finally learned to love yourself, you'll find yourself playing golf at Leisure World.

—CHARLES KRAUTHAMMER, AUTHOR
McGILL UNIVERSITY, 1993

He, who cannot rule himself, possesses no power by which he can rule his neighbor. Men of this sort, professed patriots and loud in their expressions of attachment to their country, are they, who are partisans in politics, bigots in religion, and enthusiasts in any enterprise in which self may be exalted. From this class come those who, as children and pupils, are disobedient, as citizens riotous, as soldiers insubordinate, and as officers traitors. The foundation of all excellency in action, intellectual and physical, is laid in self-control: In which the passions and desires are hushed, and the intellect, undisturbed in the silence and solitude of thoughts pursues her way and reaches the desired conclusion. . . .

—H. L. BAUGHER, PRESIDENT OF THE COLLEGE
PENNSYLVANIA COLLEGE, 1861

Whatever be your pursuits, be not satisfied with the character of being barely respectable. Let no attainment, short of eminence, content you. If you, yourselves, respect not your talents, you must not expect them to be respected by others. If you distrust your own understandings, and once persuade yourselves that you can accomplish but little; it is certain that you will accomplish but very little. Unless you aim at distinction, be assured you will never attain it. No limits are prescribed to the efforts of the understanding; and it is difficult to name the bounds, which genius and application may not surpass. Few men have ever accomplished more than they expected; and few have failed of the object, which they were determined to accomplish.

—HENRY DAVIS, PRESIDENT OF THE COLLEGE
MIDDLEBURY COLLEGE, 1810

JOBS

You are not going to "go forth." You are going to take that damn hat off and you're going to get a job.

—BILL COSBY, COMEDIAN
SOUTHERN METHODIST UNIVERSITY, 1995

You have played—now comes work. . . . And with the lifework chosen, remember that it can become, as you will it, drudgery or heroism, prosaic or romantic, brutal or divine. Who of the world today cares whether Washington was a farmer or a merchant? Who thinks of Lincoln as a country lawyer, or reads of St. Peter, the fisherman, praying to Jesus Christ, the carpenter?

—W. E. B. DU BOIS, HISTORIAN AND EDUCATOR
FISK UNIVERSITY, 1898

I asked myself, what are graduates most interested in? How to get a job? W. C. Fields, that mellow comedian for the ages, offered this advice for those looking for a job: "Never show up for an interview in bare feet, and do not read your prospective employer's mail while he is asking about your qualifications."

I would add: speak up and show some life about you. Almost anyone who can give you a decent job is half deaf.

—Liz Carpenter, journalist and author
Sam Houston State University, 1994

Accept that no matter where you go to work, you are not an employee—you are a business with one employee, you. Nobody owes you a career. You own it, as a sole proprietor. You must compete with millions of individuals every day of your career. You must enhance your value every day, hone your competitive advantage, learn, adapt, move jobs and industries—retrench so you can advance, learn new skills. So you do not become one of those statistics in 2015. And remember: This process starts on Monday.

—ANDY GROVE, CHIEF EXECUTIVE OFFICER, INTEL CORP.
HAAS SCHOOL OF BUSINESS
(UNIVERSITY OF CALIFORNIA, BERKELEY), 1994

The world quite frankly doesn't give a damn that the class of 1980 at Texas A&M is about to climb on board.... In exactly one year, in this very room and in rooms like it all across the country, there will be thousands and thousands of young men and women primed and ready to take your jobs. You have a one-year head start. Get busy.

—WILLIAM P. HOBBY, LT. GOVERNOR, TEXAS
TEXAS A&M UNIVERSITY, 1980

The men who make rapid success in their first venture in life are not numerous, and some of them are actually injured if they do.

—ABBOTT LAWRENCE LOWELL, PRESIDENT OF THE UNIVERSITY
HARVARD UNIVERSITY, 1914

It is better to start late on the right job than to spend a frustrating and mediocre life in the wrong one.

—M. T. Harrington, president, Texas A&M
Louisiana State University, 1952

Those of you going to work...my advice is: The first day, stay late.... You're going to make an impression on the janitor anyway, and that's the person who gossips.

—Bill Cosby, comedian
Lafayette College, 1996

The necessity for making a living keeps our minds so bound down to the details of professional success that we sometimes forget there is anything except professional success to live for. The necessity of conforming our habits and standards to the habits and standards of those about us, in order that we may do efficient work, makes us forget that there is a point where conformity ceases to be a virtue.

—ARTHUR TWINING HADLEY, PRESIDENT OF THE UNIVERSITY
YALE UNIVERSITY, 1906

I tell you, with the job market you're facing, you're a terrific audience.

—JERRY SEINFELD, COMEDIAN
QUEENS COLLEGE, 1994

Early betake yourselves to some profession. No thing is more debasing to the intellect or morals than that unsettled state of life which falls to the man who has nothing to do. The bare fact that his mind is unemployed is sufficient to weaken its strength, to paralyse its activity, and to dissipate its former acquisitions. And as if this was not enough, he is almost sure to fall prey to temptation, and to sink into habits of self-indulgence, which will enervate his mind, and stupify his moral sense, and bury him in an early and ignoble grave. The idle man is a wretch. Having nothing to engage his attention, his mind only preys upon itself, or sinks into a tiresome listlessness more insupportable than downright misery.

—EDWARD GRIFFIN, PRESIDENT OF THE COLLEGE
WILLIAMS COLLEGE, 1822

If you are not one of those lucky people who know exactly what they want, be very careful indeed about the kind of job you select. . . . A great many jobs, often highly paid, do people harm. You can become, for example, a more civilized and cultured person school-teaching in the sticks than typing in a New York publisher's office and going to all the good shows in the evening.

—W. H. AUDEN, POET
SMITH COLLEGE, 1940

How useful some of you may be in a particular line of work depends on whether you keep your ideas wider than your speciality.

—CLEO F. CRAIG, PRESIDENT, AT&T
UNIVERSITY OF MISSOURI, 1952

Your diploma is a passport to a world where nearly half the people have jettisoned logic, eschewed liberty, and reduced human beings by the hundreds of millions to the status of expendable gadgets.

—PHILIP WYLIE, WRITER
UNIVERSITY OF MIAMI, 1952

You see in certain ways, I envy you; for one thing, all of you know what you'll be doing next year.

—Ronald Reagan, U.S. President
U.S. Coast Guard Academy, 1988
(the end of his second term)

CHARACTER

How can anyone really be sane in America today? There is little if any occasion for one to attempt a description of our modern life. We have gone mad in our search for whatever we may be seeking! It makes little difference what the object of our endeavors may be. The spirit and method are quite the same. Whether it is wealth, fame, or education, we want to get it as quickly as possible. Whether we are building a railroad or a cathedral, writing a book or painting a picture, few Americans are willing to take time to produce a really great result. Life today is so hurried, so tense, so frenzied, that the possibility of a sane and normal life is almost precluded. The inevitable concomitant of all this hurry and intensity is that as a people we are impulsive and hysterical. Many men today who think that they are "all run down" are, as one writer has expressed it, "all wound up." We are intemperate in our pleasure and in our work. As a consequence we are superficial in much of our thinking and living. He who proposes to live a sane life must reckon with this hysteria of our day.

—MARION LE ROY BURTON, PRESIDENT OF THE COLLEGE
SMITH COLLEGE, 1914

Allured by the delusive charms of a tempting World, the Youth as he advances in years, makes excursions, extends his acquaintance, and fixes upon some object as the darling of his pursuit. He proportions the worth of everything around him, accordingly as it first strikes his imagination. All the gaieties of the world assault him at once. Pleasure allures him, riches solicit him, and honors court him. If he withstands the first attack, it is ten to one, but the second proves too powerful; he soon forms different ideas of virtue and merit, yields himself as captive and becomes a slave. Has he been taught to despise pleasure, the grand mistress of the world? The delirious, thrilling sensation, strengthened by natural fire, will soon enervate his resolution and unsinew the most confirmed purposes of reason and philosophy; unless culture has disclosed the deceitful charms.

—TIMOTHY DWIGHT, PRESIDENT OF THE COLLEGE
YALE COLLEGE, 1772

So often do you see collegians enter life with high resolve and lofty purpose and then watch them shrink and shrink to sordid, selfish, shrewd plodders, full of distrust and sneers.

—W. E. B. DU BOIS, HISTORIAN AND EDUCATOR
FISK UNIVERSITY, 1898

A man who desires to do his duty without making any sacrifices for it is like one who seeks to be a soldier without risking his life. He may parade in a uniform in time of peace, but he is not the real stuff that soldiers are made of.

—ABBOTT LAWRENCE LOWELL, PRESIDENT OF THE UNIVERSITY
HARVARD UNIVERSITY, 1911

When you want position, beware of position. But when you are called because you are worthy, when you are startled at the call you can afford to take the place in life that beckons and bids you come.

— MARTIN GROVE BRUMBAUGH, PRESIDENT OF THE COLLEGE
JUNIATA COLLEGE, 1898

If you value the world simply for what you can get out of it, be assured that the world will in turn estimate your value to it by what it can get out of you. ... If you pursue truth, people will be true to you. ...

— ARTHUR TWINING HADLEY, PRESIDENT OF THE UNIVERSITY
YALE UNIVERSITY, 1903

How generally are duellists haughty, overbearing, passionate, quarrelsome, and abusive; troublesome neighbors, uncomfortable friends, and disturbers of common happiness. Their pretentions to honour and delicacy are merely pretensions; a deplorable egotism of character which precludes them from all enjoyment, and prevents those around them from possessing quiet, and comfort, unless every thing is conformed to their vain and capricious demand.

There is neither delicacy nor honour, in giving or taking affronts easily and suddenly, nor in justifying them on the one hand, nor in revenging them on the other. Very little children do all these things daily, without either honour or delicacy, from the mere impulse of infantile passion. Those who imitate them in this conduct, resemble them in character; and are only bigger children.

—FROM "A SERMON ON DUELLING"
TIMOTHY DWIGHT, PRESIDENT OF THE COLLEGE
YALE COLLEGE, 1804

If those who are best equipped to think deeply, and to form public opinion wisely, think loosely or advocate opinions that are inaccurate, unbalanced, and unsound, the people are in danger. An individual may win fame quickly by new and eccentric views, but for the public it is far more important that his ideas should be correct than that they should be startling.

—ABBOTT LAWRENCE LOWELL, PRESIDENT OF THE UNIVERSITY HARVARD UNIVERSITY, 1911

When life does get tough and the crisis is undeniably at hand, when we must, in an instant, look inward for strength of character to see us through, we will find nothing inside ourselves that we have not already put there.

—RONALD REAGAN, U.S. PRESIDENT
THE CITADEL, 1993

Remember that the sense of imperilment, the sense of danger, the sense of your values and your best selves being threatened at every moment by indifference, by coarseness, by apathy, and necessity, is in fact your greatest ally. It is against these forces, the great multitudinous, anonymous modern abyss that your personal values are defined as what they are. It is at the edge, on the brink, that your essences show themselves as they must be. So I say develop your private brinkmanship, your strategies, your ruses, your delightful and desperate games of inner survival . . . ones that will enable you to live perpetually at the edge, but there very much on your own ground, and to live there with personal style, with dash, and with verve and a distinct and exhilarating sense of existing on your terms as they develop, or as they become, with time, more and more what they always have been.

—JAMES DICKEY, POET
PITZER COLLEGE, 1965
(Addressed to the three young women who
constituted Pitzer's first graduating class)

The best talent thrives only on what is hard.

—CLEO F. CRAIG, PRESIDENT, AT&T
UNIVERSITY OF MISSOURI, 1952

Some maudlin statements of present-day pursuers of office have jumbled Henry Clay's phrase and seem to be saying, "I would rather be President than be right!"

—REV. JAMES MCLEOD, CHAPLAIN, NORTHWESTERN UNIVERSITY
MIDDLEBURY COLLEGE, 1952

Remember when you hear yourself saying one day that you don't have time anymore to read or listen to music or look at paintings or go to the movies or do whatever feeds your head now. Then you're getting old. That means they got you, after all. I wish you love, courage, and fantasy.

—SUSAN SONTAG, WRITER
WELLESLEY COLLEGE, 1983

INSPIRATIONS

Above all, I have learned from the most inspiring force of my life, my husband King Hussein, who assumed his responsibilities at an age most of you entered university.

—QUEEN NOOR OF JORDAN
AMERICAN UNIVERSITY,
1995

I was fourteen years old the night my daddy died. He had holes in his shoes and a vision that he was able to convey to me even lying in an ambulance, dying, that I as a black girl could do and be anything, that race and gender are shadows, and that character, determination, attitude are the substances of life.

... The clear childhood message I internalized was that as God's child, no man or woman could look down on me and I could look down on no man or woman.

—MARIAN WRIGHT EDELMAN,
PRESIDENT, CHILDREN'S DEFENSE FUND
HOWARD UNIVERSITY, 1990

Why are heroines and even heroes so out of fashion? Nobility of purpose is not currently admired; our society is afraid that following such a leader will extract too high a cost from us as individuals or as a nation. Rather, we deny greatness and seek instead a false image of equality. In our compulsive effort to make everyone ordinary we assume license to delve into personal matters, from the trivial to the profound; unsurprisingly, the glorious images are tarnished. And for those who are truly great, where the effort to make them ordinary cannot succeed, we strive to make them evil. Not even the giants of our world can escape. Consider the sad efforts to tarnish Martin Luther King's image, as if that could undermine his greatness.

...People have always known that heroines and heroes are imperfect. But they chose to ignore the warts so that the greatness could inspire new achievement....

Young women now have more freedom to shape themselves than young women anywhere or at anytime in history. That freedom is a lonely and difficult burden, but it is also a blessing. The burden cannot be conquered nor the blessing realized by standing in anyone's shadow. But both can be achieved by standing on the shoulders of the great heroines.

—MAXINE SINGER, PRESIDENT,
CARNEGIE INSTITUTION OF WASHINGTON
BARNARD COLLEGE, 1991

Abraham Lincoln did not go to Gettysburg having commissioned a poll to find out what would sell in Gettysburg. There were no people with percentages for him, cautioning him about this group or that group or what they found in exit polls a year earlier. When will we have the courage of Lincoln?

—ROBERT COLES, EDUCATOR AND
PULITZER PRIZE–WINNING AUTHOR
BELOIT COLLEGE, 1984

I was thinking—just as an example of how much the times influence what a person does with his life—if Abraham Lincoln were alive today, would he be standing here making his Gettysburg Address? Of course not. Lincoln would probably be a relatively obscure lawyer who was turned down for the Supreme Court because he and Mary had a live-in maid for whom they never paid Social Security.

—ANDY ROONEY, JOURNALIST AND HUMORIST
GETTYSBURG COLLEGE, 1994

Get mad at anybody who tells you you have to settle for less. Tell them, get the hell out of my way! To the class of '85, start your engines.

—LEE IACOCCA, AUTOMOBILE INDUSTRY EXECUTIVE
MIT, 1985

I hope that you'll remember, even when you're feeling blue, that it's you I like, it's you yourself, it's you.

—Fred Rogers ("Mister Rogers"), television host
University of South Carolina, 1985

A usable mind is a most exciting possession. You have discovered that. To use your own mind is the high privilege of men who are really free.

—Mildred McAfee Horton, president of the college
Wellesley College, 1949

Unless people like you give us a new generation, willing to take on the challenge of self-government, willing to accept its responsibilities, to reform it, to change it, to make it fairer and more responsive—unless you do, the very rich will get richer, the poor will become fixed in their desperation, violence will increase, and here, as in so many places around the world, the purpose of government will be reduced basically to a matter of maintaining order instead of improving conditions.... You must recognize that you can make a difference.

—MARIO CUOMO, GOVERNOR OF NEW YORK
UNIVERSITY OF ROCHESTER, 1985

I have the courage to act because I so profoundly believe that you and your generation—breathing down my back eager to seize the reins from my hands—will modify the contribution I and my generation will make.... This is why we are so dependent on the corrective and often disruptive power of your own inexperience.... The old may very often be the very best professionals, but only the young, the un-initiated, can play the role of the very bright amateurs who ask the brash and sometimes rash questions opening up new vistas and new possibilities for man and men.

—JACQUELINE GRENNAN, EDUCATOR
SKIDMORE COLLEGE, 1967

Belief is the supreme power of the soul; unbelief its supreme wickedness. No faculty gives us the range of the spiritual universe but this, the faculty of faith. If we walk by sight only, we can never pass those bounds which divide the visible and the invisible, the present and the future, the mortal and the immortal.

—John Bascom, president of the university
University of Wisconsin, 1874

There is a great difference between information and inspiration. You can get information by the cartful and the wagonful and the libraryful and the Sunday newspaperful, or in any other chunks or lumps that you choose. It is as common as rocks and bricks. Information you can get; if one has no time to buy it he can go and hire another man to get it for him as one secures the services of the lawyer or the doctor. One can get information either from books or from men. It is cheap; it is common; and it is worth about as much as it costs. But inspiration which comes from touching the life of truth itself is a priceless gem which comes only from close, devoted and continuous toil. A man knows when he has touched red-hot truth. He feels the shock. . . .

—Martin Grove Brumbaugh, president of the college
Juniata College, 1898

WHO? ME?

I've been trying to figure out why they asked me to give this address. What valuable life lessons did they hope I could offer? What did they anticipate I would talk about? All I can figure is: they must want me to talk about what I know best. So I have titled today's commencement address: "How to Become a Movie Star."

—Geena Davis, movie actress
New England College, 1992

I am famous. That is a large part of why I was asked to speak here today.... It is a large part of the reason I received an honorary doctorate today when in fact I don't even have a bachelor's degree—because I'm famous. I would like to think that it's also because I'm a pretty good guy and I'm passionate about my craft and my business, but it's not. It's because I'm famous and the funny thing is that my fame is a complete accident.... Fame, this thing that I have, is very rare, very strange, and very meaningless. It is a poor measure of success.... Look beyond the veneer of what you consider success. I would like you to try to focus now and for the rest of your lives not on glory but greatness.

—JASON ALEXANDER, ACTOR
SCHOOL OF THE ARTS, 1995

I was like probably most of you. I did not graduate Summa Cum Laude or Magna Cum Laude, I graduated, Oh Thank You Lordy!

—ANDREW YOUNG, MAYOR OF ATLANTA
UNIVERSITY OF NOTRE DAME, 1987

I've played nuns and hookers, but I've never worn a gown like this.

—LYNN REDGRAVE, ACTRESS
BARUCH COLLEGE, 1995

As a college student, I was never on any dean's honor roll. In fact ... the university I attended showed a strange lack of interest in having me continue as a member of its student body.

—PAUL HOFFMAN, ECA CORPORATION CHAIRMAN
WASHINGTON UNIVERSITY, 1949
(HOFFMAN LEFT THE UNIVERSITY OF CHICAGO AFTER
FRESHMAN YEAR TO SELL CARS. IN 1949, ECA CORPORATION
WAS THE 7TH LARGEST COMPANY IN THE WORLD.)

I tried, just for fun, to remember who spoke at my college commencement seventeen years ago, and I must tell you, I have no idea.

—ALBERT GORE, JR., SENATOR
TUSCULUM COLLEGE, 1986

It's not surprising in the years to come that you will not recall this commencement speaker, but his name is not easy to pronounce.

—Daniel Inouye, senator
George Washington University, 1989

Let me put your minds at ease. I will not be speaking about pickup trucks, NASCAR racing, or bass fishing. My text contains no rebel yells, is totally devoid of the word "redneck," and I definitely will not be taking requests.

—Charlie Daniels, country music performer
University of North Carolina at Wilmington, 1996

SECRETS

A lot of people have been quoting me ever since I came to play for the Yankees in 1946. But, as I once said, I really didn't say everything I said. So now it's my turn to give some of my famous advice to the graduates. First, never give up, because it's never over till it's over. Second, during the years ahead, when you come to a fork in the road, take it. Third, don't always follow the crowd, because nobody goes there anymore. It's too crowded. Fourth, stay alert. You can observe a lot by watching. Fifth, and last, remember that whatever you do in life, ninety percent of it is half mental.

—YOGI BERRA,
HALL OF FAME BASEBALL CATCHER, AND MANAGER
MONTCLAIR STATE UNIVERSITY, 1996

Life itself depends upon the power of the human soul to know things that elude it.

—MARTIN GROVE BRUMBAUGH, PRESIDENT OF THE COLLEGE
JUNIATA COLLEGE, 1898

What Moses brought down from Mount Sinai were not the Ten Suggestions.

—TED KOPPEL, JOURNALIST
DUKE UNIVERSITY, 1987

Wandering is one of the most sensible things in the world to do. I highly recommend the pursuit of happiness from east to west, bending and stopping, pausing, enjoying, not going anywhere in particular except down a beach or around a pond, always knowing that there is something wonderful just ahead. City street or country lane, for the naturalist there is always something to see: lichen puddled on the granite, a new fern frond uncurling like a mainspring, a pad of brilliant green moss studded with scarlet mite. Ask why, and for every question you answer you'll have a bouquet of another dozen questions. And herein lies sanity.

—ANN H. ZWINGER, NATURALIST AND AUTHOR
CARLETON COLLEGE, 1984

Unless each day can be looked back upon by an individual as one in which he has had some fun, some joy, some real satisfaction, that day is a loss.

—DWIGHT D. EISENHOWER, U.S. PRESIDENT
DARTMOUTH COLLEGE, 1953

We do not change as we grow up. The difference between the child and the adult is that the former doesn't know who he is and the latter does.

—W. H. AUDEN, POET
SMITH COLLEGE, 1940

Let not the Lapses or ridiculous Accidents or Behaviours of Men in Drink or in Love be taken notice of after, or upbraided to them in jest or earnest, for no man loves to have his folly remembered, nor have the Consequence of Wine or Passion imputed to him. . . .

When you borrow, chuse rather a rich creditor and a great Debt, than many trifling Debts dispersed among poor People; a poor man's little Debt makes the most noise. Defer therefore not to pay Mechanicks, etc., their utmost Dues, for they are craving and clamorous, & consider only your Condition in the world, not your present Exigence. . . .

—from *LETTER OF ADVICE TO A YOUNG GENTLEMAN UPON LEAVING THE UNIVERSITY CONCERNING HIS BEHAVIOUR AND CONVERSATION IN THE WORLD*, by R.L. NEW YORK, 1696

Leave nothing undone which ought to be done; do nothing which ought to be omitted. Let the transitory vanities, the visionary enjoyments of time fleet by you, unnoticed. Point all of your views to the elevated scenes of an immortal existence, and remember that this life is but the dawn of your being.

—TIMOTHY DWIGHT, PRESIDENT OF THE COLLEGE
YALE COLLEGE, 1776

You'll have some regrets along with the happy memories. I let football and other extracurricular activities eat into my study time with the result that my grade-point average was closer to the C level required for eligibility than it was to straight A's. And even now I wonder what I would've accomplished if I'd studied harder.

—RONALD REAGAN, U.S. PRESIDENT
EUREKA COLLEGE, 1982
(EUREKA WAS HIS ALMA MATER)

What's the trick? There are three of them: A sense of real purpose, a sense of humor, and a sense of constant curiosity. Keep using those to the grave because learning really never ends.

—LIZ CARPENTER, JOURNALIST AND AUTHOR
SAM HOUSTON STATE UNIVERSITY, 1994

If you turn up forty, drunk and maudlin at parties talking about how great everything was when you were in school, man, you are one sick puppy.

—STEPHEN KING, WRITER
UNIVERSITY OF MAINE, 1987

Opportunity is like a hair on a bald-headed man; it only comes around once and you have to grab it while it's there.

> —JOYCELYN ELDERS, FORMER U.S. SURGEON GENERAL
> BROWN UNIVERSITY, 1995

Liberal knowledge gives dignity to the mind. Dignity of mind is always attended with a spirit of liberty.

> —LEONARD WOODS, VALEDICTORIAN
> HARVARD COLLEGE, 1796

My one piece of advice is to keep your sense of humor above all.... We now have self-cartooning politicians. I mean if you proposed a cartoon in which a vice president tries to blame a billion-dollar riot on a television sitcom no one would print it. Editors would ask, "Where do you get these crazy ideas?"

Life is, after all, essentially a joke. If you don't think so, look at the hats you're wearing.

—JEFF DANZIGER, EDITORIAL CARTOONIST,
THE *CHRISTIAN SCIENCE MONITOR*
MIDDLEBURY COLLEGE, 1992

The nature of all classes of men is the same; and polished persons will do the same things which are done by clowns. . . .

—TIMOTHY DWIGHT, PRESIDENT OF THE COLLEGE
YALE COLLEGE, 1804

Whatever you got, it's in here, see [pointing to his heart]. Don't worry about the clown suit and the makeup and the nose. But when you get out there just be the best you can and keep your mind on your routine.

—LOU JACOBS, VETERAN CLOWN
CLOWN COLLEGE, FLORIDA, 1982

I don't know whether this is the best of times or the worst of times, but I assure you it's the only time you've got. You can either sit on your expletive deleted or pick a daisy.

—ART BUCHWALD, HUMORIST
UNIVERSITY OF SAN DIEGO, 1976

Be different—if you don't have the facts and knowledge required, simply listen. When word gets around that you can listen when others tend to talk, you will be treated as a sage.

—ED KOCH, FORMER MAYOR OF NEW YORK CITY
ROGER WILLIAMS UNIVERSITY, 1996

The sixth sense is good sense and none other.

—M. WOOLSEY STRYKER, PRESIDENT OF THE COLLEGE
HAMILTON COLLEGE, 1893

Few virtues are more important to society than general cleanliness. It ought to be carefully cultivated everywhere; but in populous cities it should almost be revered.

—JAMES ABERCROMBIE, PRESIDENT OF THE ACADEMY
PHILADELPHIA ACADEMY, 1810

Progress is not inevitably upward and onward.

—REV. LOUIS HADLEY EVANS, EDUCATOR
UNIVERSITY OF KANSAS, 1952

As I think back and look forward, I see how nothing is unambiguous; nothing is without risk. Salvation does not come through simplicities.

—A. BARTLETT GIAMMATI, PRESIDENT OF THE UNIVERSITY
YALE UNIVERSITY, 1986

Born, as I was, in obscurity, a stranger to the halls of learning, environed by ignorance, degradation, and their concomitants, from birth to manhood, I do not feel at liberty to mark out, with any degree of confidence, or dogmatism, what is the precise vocation of the Scholar. Yet this I *can* say, as a denizen of the world, and as a citizen of a country rolling in the sin and shame of slavery, the most flagrant and scandalous that ever saw the sun, "Whatsoever things are true, whatsoever things are honest, whatsoever things are just, whatsoever things are pure, whatsoever things are lovely, whatsoever things are of good report, if there be any virtue, and there be any praise, think on these things."

—FREDERICK DOUGLASS, ABOLITIONIST
WESTERN RESERVE COLLEGE, 1854

Imagination without hard work is usually barren; and what is more, the brighter the imagination the greater the amount of work required to its full fruition.

—ABBOTT LAWRENCE LOWELL, PRESIDENT OF THE UNIVERSITY
HARVARD UNIVERSITY, 1910

Being twenty-something is all about taking it in— eating it, drinking it, and spitting out the seeds later. It's about being fearless, and stupid, and dangerous, and unfocused, and abandoned. It's about being in it, not on top of it.

—JODIE FOSTER, FILM ACTRESS AND DIRECTOR
YALE UNIVERSITY, 1993

Be careful what you swallow. Chew!

—Gwendolyn Brooks, poet
Buena Vista University, 1995

There might be false starts and do-overs. You are
entitled to experiment before you find your calling.
Look at Sonny Bono.

—Jane Pauley, journalist
Providence College, 1995

I will now give you your last lesson in metaphysics—
nothing is as real as a dream. The world can change
about you, but your dream will not. It will always be
the link with the person you are today, young and
full of hope. If you hold on to it you may grow old
but you will never be old. And that, ladies and gentlemen, is the ultimate success.

—TOM CLANCY, AUTHOR
VILLANOVA UNIVERSITY, 1990

Ask questions.

—SUSAN SARANDON, ACTRESS
RUTGERS COLLEGE, 1993

The influence of method in the economy of human life is as wonderful in its effect as that of habit.... This reflection naturally leads me to suggest to you another essential branch of duty, viz., *punctuality with respect to all appointed duties and engagements.*

Punctuality promotes despatch in the performance of business, and prevents an unjust trespass upon the time, the avocations, and the patience of the individual with whom the appointment is made; and also rescues from inactivity those hours which would otherwise be wasted in the tedium of expectation, the insipidity of idleness, or the censures of the other party. Every breach of punctuality, besides being an infringement of moral obligation, is moreover a gross violation of the laws of good breeding and politeness. Be therefore upon all occasions scrupulously and rigidly attentive to the fulfillment of all your engagements, and endeavor always to be a little before rather than one minute after the time specified.

—JAMES ABERCROMBIE, PRESIDENT OF THE ACADEMY
PHILADELPHIA ACADEMY, 1810

An over-deference to tradition will not do the trick.

—WILLIAM CARLSON, PRESIDENT
STATE UNIVERSITY OF NEW YORK
BROOKLYN POLYTECHNICAL INSTITUTE, 1952

I would advise you to keep your overhead down;
avoid a major drug habit; play every day.

—JAMES TAYLOR, MUSICIAN
BERKLEE COLLEGE OF MUSIC, 1995

In playing ball, or in life, a person occasionally gets the opportunity to do something great. When that time comes, only two things matter: being prepared to seize the moment and having the courage to take your best swing.

—HANK AARON, FORMER BASEBALL PLAYER,
GENERAL MANAGER OF THE ATLANTA BRAVES
EMORY UNIVERSITY SCHOOL OF LAW, 1995

One thing I want to tell you that only a non-doctor can tell you and that is that the head-bone is connected to the heart-bone. Don't ever let them come apart.

—ALAN ALDA, ACTOR
COLUMBIA MEDICAL SCHOOL, 1979

Words such as belief and perseverance and quality often seem meaningless and hard to come by these days.... Learn to know what's best and insist on it.

—HELEN FRANKENTHALER, ARTIST
CITY COLLEGE OF NEW YORK, 1995

Avoid fatty foods. Avoid smoking, drugs, Benson-hurst, the Gaza Strip, bungee jumping, humorless people, bad music, fashion, weight training, and hair-care products.

—CHEVY CHASE, ACTOR
BARD COLLEGE, 1990

That is a slow process by which enlargement comes to man in his apprehension of himself, and of his wider relations. At his birth he is often spoken of as a stranger. He is a stranger in a strange world—how strange!—but to no one is he a greater stranger than to himself. How little does the infant know or suspect of the capacities that are in him for apprehension, for joy and suffering, for varied emotion and passion, for action, and for an eternal duration. . . . And few men, if any, learn, during a lifetime, their own capacities. Among the last things that a man comes to know thoroughly, is himself.

—MARK HOPKINS, PRESIDENT OF THE COLLEGE
WILLIAMS COLLEGE, 1863

Be willing to make decisions. That's the most important quality in a good leader. Don't fall victim to what I call the "ready-aim-aim-aim-aim syndrome." You must be willing to fire.

—T. BOONE PICKENS, BUSINESSMAN
GEORGE WASHINGTON UNIVERSITY, 1988

It is always difficult to be meaningful and relevant, because there's just not enough time. Time to think seriously is hard to come by.

I have been working all this past week in Los Angeles on a new television pilot prime-time series. I left the taping at three o'clock this morning your time, chartered a plane, and flew all morning to get here by ten. So I just want to tell you, if I fall asleep don't worry, don't panic, and don't disturb me.

—OPRAH WINFREY, TELEVISION HOST
TENNESSEE STATE UNIVERSITY, 1987

God was under no obligation to call you into being; or to assign you so dignified a rank among his creatures. . . . It is owing solely to his sovereign and unmerited goodness, that you are blessed with the light of life; that you bear on your souls his glorious image; and that you resemble, in understanding, the angels in his presence.

—HENRY DAVIS, PRESIDENT OF THE COLLEGE
MIDDLEBURY COLLEGE, 1810

SUCCESS

You may succeed in the lower sense of that word. You may become rich; may come to be the first man in a village, or a member of Congress, or the Governor of a State, or the President of the United States, and may suppose yourselves to be engaged, as ten thousand have before you, in the most important and momentous concerns that have ever transpired. But, however high you may rise, you will be borne up by a wave that has risen quite as high before, and when it subsides it will strand you where it has stranded others, and leave you to neglect, while the popular gaze is waiting for him who is to succeed you.

—MARK HOPKINS, PRESIDENT OF THE COLLEGE
WILLIAMS COLLEGE, 1872

In a country where "all men are created equal," the acquisition of wealth will ever be a prime object of universal attention... every individual is convinced that his importance, respectability, and influence in society must result either from his abilities, his virtues, or his property. As the latter is much more easily attainable, and unfortunately in much higher estimation, than either of the former, we cannot be greatly surprised to find its votaries so numerous, so indefatigable, and so successful.

—JOSEPH PERKINS, PROFESSOR
HARVARD COLLEGE, 1797

Where, alas, is the great and good man, that has not been abused? Where the Roman patriot, that was not disgraced? Where the Grecian savior, that had not his virtue attested and his glory established by exile? We may therefore hold up to others this encouragement: if you will serve your country faithfully; if you will do more good, than any other man, you may expect, as a reward, enmity and scandal. If we look into any age or nation, we shall find that merit begat glory, glory begat envy, envy begat jealousy, jealousy begat falsehood, falsehood begat faction.

—LEONARD WOODS, VALEDICTORIAN
HARVARD COLLEGE, 1796

What actor has not accepted hundreds of Academy Awards in his living room and bathroom holding a toothbrush as the little Oscar statue? Success and fame and all of their rewards, that is what you want. ...In short, you want what I have.

—Jason Alexander, actor
School of the Arts, 1995

If you want to waste a perfectly wonderful lifetime becoming filthy rich, at least have the good sense not to offend the neighbors by praising your own selfishness. Neighbors are the kind of people who do jury duty.

—Russell Baker, columnist
University of Miami, 1990

It is not enough for a man to be greater that his appetites and greater than his ambitions; he must be greater than his works. . . . It is not the startling deeds that make the man, but the character which is behind them. . . . The greatest things that a man can do are quite as likely to result from his failures as from his successes.

—ARTHUR TWINING HADLEY, PRESIDENT OF THE UNIVERSITY
   YALE UNIVERSITY, 1902

BREVITY IS THE SOUL OF WIT

I know that I am pretty popular as a commencement speaker largely because I'm brief.

—Maya Angelou, poet
North Carolina State University, 1990

I know you degree candidates are wondering, even some of your parents and friends in the audience— who are so rightly proud of you today, are wondering: how long am I going to take?

—Rodney Ellis, Texas state senator
University of Houston, 1994

To try to talk to the young people who will run the future of our society, in ten minutes, is a little like trying to put a cantaloupe in a Coke bottle.

—QUINCY JONES, MUSICIAN, ENTERTAINMENT EXECUTIVE
CLAREMONT GRADUATE SCHOOL, 1995

Feelings. Adventures. Ideas.

—RICHARD MOORE, PRESIDENT OF SANTA MONICA COLLEGE
CROSSROADS SCHOOL FOR ARTS AND SCIENCES, 1992

(This was Moore's entire speech. He shortened his remarks because nearly a dozen speakers had preceded him. He received a standing ovation.)

I will be brief. Not nearly as brief as Salvador Dali, who gave the world's shortest speech. He said, "I will be so brief I have already finished," and he sat down.

—EDWARD O. WILSON, BIOLOGIST
PENN STATE UNIVERSITY, 1995

I know it's been four tough grueling years. Now, my friends, comes the hard part. You're going to sit through my commencement address.

—DAN QUAYLE, U.S. VICE PRESIDENT
U.S. MILITARY ACADEMY, 1989

I understand you people with the earphones staying plugged in to the baseball game. If I were sitting up there I would be doing exactly the same thing.

—GEORGE BUSH, U.S. PRESIDENT
MISSISSIPPI STATE UNIVERSITY, 1989

I will try to follow the advice that a university president once gave a prospective commencement speaker. "Think of yourself as the body at an Irish wake," he said. "They need you in order to have the party, but nobody expects you to say very much."

—NATIONAL SECURITY ADVISER ANTHONY LAKE
(AND MANY, MANY OTHERS)
UNIVERSITY OF MASSACHUSETTS, 1995

We ask for assurances that when we die as individuals, as we must, mankind will live on. Well, I can see that many of you have stopped listening.

—WALTER MONDALE, FORMER U.S. VICE PRESIDENT
SARAH LAWRENCE COLLEGE, 1982

The ancient and honorable custom of commencement speeches is really an innocuous one that has done very little harm to those who are graduating, and it may even have the beneficial consequence of teaching you the virtue of patience.

—WARREN BURGER, U.S. SUPREME COURT CHIEF JUSTICE
PACE UNIVERSITY, 1983

Just a few minutes ago, all of us heard the chairman of your board say that no one sleeps through a Notre Dame graduation. I regard that as a personal challenge.

—DEREK BOK, PRESIDENT, HARVARD UNIVERSITY
UNIVERSITY OF NOTRE DAME, 1987

PREDICTIONS

We have uncovered a universe brimming over with wonders. We are on our way, if we are not so foolish as to destroy ourselves first, to the planets and to the stars. Which path we take, which destiny we choose is up to us. . . . All future generations, if there are any, will look back to this time as a fundamental crossroads in human history. The choice, I believe, is literally between life and death.

—CARL SAGAN, ASTRONOMER
UNIVERSITY OF SOUTH CAROLINA, 1984

Science and technology hold out for you a dazzling and almost unimaginable future. At the same time, science and technology hold out an alternative future, unimaginable, too, but endlessly, illimitably dark.

—ARTHUR SCHLESINGER, HISTORIAN
SAN DIEGO UNIVERSITY, 1983

It is conceivable that someday we will build a robot that will learn, that will show some of the things that are typically human such as insight, intuition, creativity, inspiration. But even if we do, it would be so troublesome, so difficult, we would have to put so much into it, that it wouldn't be cost-effective. It wouldn't be worth our while. Human beings can do it so easily.

—ISAAC ASIMOV, AUTHOR
ITHACA COLLEGE, 1983

A robot is only an extension of the human body, and to meet the future demand for challenges the human body will have to expand its energies.

—"ROBOT REDFORD"
ANNE ARUNDEL COMMUNITY COLLEGE, 1983

("Redford" was a 4-foot-tall fiberglass robot from Superior Robotics of America in California. It "looked at" the audience and displayed the view on a television monitor in its chest. It "spoke" via remote control. The robot's owner, William Bakaleinikoff, wrote its speech. He, and it, received the graduates' enthusiastic applause.)

I'm sure you all feel like I do, that there is sort of an underlying chaos to daily life and maybe it has something to do with the approaching millennium. . . . It feels to me like we actually are on some kind of brink here. Of course, America's always had this sort of weird and idiosyncratic nature to pull itself from the fire right at the brink. . . . I've heard this cry from this new generation that's coming on, that there's a dispirit about the future because opportunity and jobs have been robbed by the greedy generation that came before. . . . I still have genuine hope for the future because my hope is not, at the moment anyway, with the leadership of this country. It's with you.

—ROBERT REDFORD, ACTOR
CLAREMONT GRADUATE SCHOOL, CALIFORNIA, 1995

A world in which eight hundred million people are starving is not safe for anyone—and that is what we could face, all too probably by the end of this century.

—KATHARINE GRAHAM,
BOARD CHAIRMAN OF THE WASHINGTON POST COMPANY
UNIVERSITY OF MARYLAND, 1980

Whether most Americans like it or not, they must face up to the stark reality that the destiny of the world will no longer be shaped exclusively or solely by persons with white skins.

—A. LEON HIGGINBOTHAM, JR., JUDGE,
U.S. COURT OF APPEALS, THIRD CIRCUIT
HOWARD UNIVERSITY, 1980

You in your lifetime, in this country, will vote for and elect a woman as president of the United States.

—PETER UEBERROTH, BUSINESSMAN
NOTRE DAME, 1989

I can confidently say to you that you will live to see a black man or woman take the oval office as president of the United States.

—DR. LOUIS SULLIVAN,
SECRETARY OF HEALTH AND HUMAN SERVICES
JACKSON STATE UNIVERSITY, 1989

I am pessimistic about our preparation for the twenty-first century. I think most people today are caught up in seeking power and status, and have forgotten justice, fairness, and decency.... I don't see enough anger and righteous indignation in this part of the twentieth century to give me hope that things will improve in the twenty-first century.

—PATRICIA ROBERTS HARRIS,
    FORMER SECRETARY OF HEALTH AND HUMAN SERVICES
    SCRIPPS COLLEGE, 1984

No matter what you read in the newspapers and see on television, we are all going to make it. For two hundred years, this country has muddled through one crisis after another, and we have done it without changing our form of government.

—ADMIRAL WILLIAM CROWE, JOINT CHIEFS OF STAFF
    UNIVERSITY OF OKLAHOMA, 1986

PARENTS

Your parents left you a perfect world. Don't louse it up.

—ART BUCHWALD, JOURNALIST
NEW YORK UNIVERSITY, 1970

When my parents were pushing me to become a doctor, I could have at least said to them, "All right, all right. Just let me tell jokes to strangers in nightclubs for eighteen years, and I'm sure after that they'll make me a doctor."

—JERRY SEINFELD, COMEDIAN
(RECEIVING HONORARY DOCTORATE FROM HIS ALMA MATER)
QUEENS COLLEGE, 1994

I'd like to begin by acknowledging a special group of people with us today—the broke but happy parents.

—GEORGE BUSH, U.S. PRESIDENT
THE COLLEGE OF WILLIAM AND MARY, 1995

[As to] how I achieved my position in the business world. . . . I can only say the easiest way is to pick parents who already own a successful business.

—STEVE FORBES, PRESIDENT AND CEO OF FORBES, INC.,
MILLIONAIRE AND PRESIDENTIAL WANNA-BE
CENTENARY COLLEGE, 1996

Sometimes we need to fuse our lives again with those people who seem at times to be antagonists—you young men especially, because it is hard for us men to profess our love. It is quite often very difficult for your fathers and for you. So for you young men, when the ceremony is over, I want you to run over to the old man. Grab him, hug him, and kiss him and say, "Dad, I love you and I thank you for all the years." That's part of the ceremony. I demand that of you when this is all over. It will save you a lot of trouble getting to know your father ten years from now.

—Ray Bradbury, writer
Harvey Mudd College, 1987

We've always been a step behind in bringing you up. ... We wanted to bring you up with information about sex that we never had. Our parents only told us that if we listened to rock 'n' roll, we would have babies—and they were right. You are them.

—GARRISON KEILLOR, COMEDIAN, AUTHOR
GETTYSBURG COLLEGE, 1987

No career [is] more urgent for a little while to come than the career of tolerating your parents ... it will soon give way to the even more challenging occupation of tolerating your children.

—ALISTAIR COOKE, EDITOR, BROADCASTER
SMITH COLLEGE, 1954

A funeral is very much like a graduation ceremony. Both are formal occasions to mark a change in status, both are times for reflection and contemplation and celebration, and both are opportunities for the young to learn from the lessons of the old as they begin to replace them. And, both are times for relatives to reassess their finances.

—Kay Bailey Hutchison, U.S. senator
Texas A&M University, 1994

OTHER VOICES

Woody Allen once offered the following advice to a graduating class: "Two paths lie ahead of you. One leads to utter despair, and the other to total extinction. May you have the wisdom to choose wisely."

—BILL BRADLEY, SENATOR
TRENTON STATE COLLEGE, 1988

I offer the wise words of the Maharani of Jaipur. She said, "Keep an open mind. An open mind is a very good thing. But don't keep your mind so open that your brains fall out."

—WILLIAM BENNETT, SECRETARY OF EDUCATION
THE CITADEL, 1986

One of the Rabbinic "Saying of the Fathers" declared, "It is not thy duty to complete the work, but neither art thou free to desist from it."

—ABBOTT LAWRENCE LOWELL, PRESIDENT OF THE UNIVERSITY
HARVARD UNIVERSITY, 1914

"Life is an adventure or nothing at all." Helen Keller, born blind, mute, deaf, said that . . . Life is an adventure or nothing at all. And she made it despite her handicaps.

—LIZ CARPENTER, JOURNALIST AND AUTHOR
SAM HOUSTON STATE UNIVERSITY, 1994

Let us realize the fragility of the planet, and our obligations to it.... Buckminster Fuller said, "The most important fact about spaceship Earth is an instruction book didn't come with it." He was right. So it is up to us to make the instruction book ... and then to follow it.

—JAMES CORBRIDGE, CHANCELLOR OF THE UNIVERSITY
UNIVERSITY OF COLORADO, 1992

The difference between average people and great people can be explained in three words. The three words are: "and then some." The top people did what was expected, and then some.

—SENATE MAJORITY LEADER BOB DOLE,
QUOTING FORMER SECRETARY OF STATE JAMES BYRNES
GALLAUDET COLLEGE, 1996

I think T. S. Eliot was absolutely right when he wrote in 1919 that tradition is not something you inherit. If you want it, you must obtain it with great labor.

—CORNEL WEST, HARVARD UNIVERSITY PROFESSOR
HAVERFORD COLLEGE, 1994

In the first place, be kind. In the second place, be kind. And in the third place, be kind. [Quoting novelist Henry James.]

—ROBERT COLES,
EDUCATOR AND PULITZER PRIZE–WINNING AUTHOR
OBERLIN COLLEGE, 1996

"Have the courage for the most extraordinary, the most singular, and the most inexplicable that we may encounter. . . . Perhaps everything terrible is in its deepest being something helpless that wants help from us." With these words of Rilke's to a young poet, I take my leave of you, wishing you all the courage of which he speaks.

—W. H. AUDEN, POET
SMITH COLLEGE, 1940

The old give the young good advice because they are no longer able to set them a bad example, says a French epigram.

—DR. LEONARD BROCKINGTON, PRESIDENT,
J. ARTHUR RANK FILM COMPANIES
MIDDLEBURY COLLEGE, 1952

A WOMAN'S PLACE . . .

Our high and mighty Lords...have denied us the means of knowledge, and then reproached us for the want of it....They doom'd the sex to servile or frivolous employments, on purpose to degrade their minds, that they themselves might hold unrivall'd, the power and eminence they had usurped. Happily, a more liberal way of thinking begins to prevail. The sources of knowledge are gradually opening to our sex.

—ANONYMOUS SPEAKER
POOR'S LADIES ACADEMY, 1794

I have no idea where we are going....Those of you who plan to be housewives may find yourselves without houses, or with a house without being a wife.

—MILDRED MCAFEE HORTON, PRESIDENT OF THE COLLEGE
WELLESLEY COLLEGE, 1949

[H]ere in America, where they [women] have already such a preponderating influence and—what is more—where they are already so conscious of their power and have begun to enjoy the satisfaction of using it, the possibilities arising out of ever-increasing numerical superiority are quite considerable . . . [T]he morality of the race depends on the morality of the womenfolk.

—HERBERT SMITH, FORMER PRESIDENT OF THE COLLEGE
SMITH COLLEGE, 1950

Never has the scholar been more needed than now, to make good marriages and good families.... Your children will need a constantly increasing source of knowledge; your husband will need a wife who is a wise and resourceful companion.... It is high time the young college woman realized that she must mobilize her trained mind, and take an active part in the politics of her neighborhood.

—MILLICENT MCINTOSH, PRESIDENT, BARNARD COLLEGE
NEW JERSEY COLLEGE FOR WOMEN, 1952

[T]he fortune of many of you here is being decided by anonymous young men who are packing their bags in New Haven, Connecticut. . . . Fate has already started to weave a web of romance, and insurance policies and diapers around many here and many so far unidentified young men, who this summer or next will be all the more susceptible to capture because they are at that age when they don't know what ails them.

—ALISTAIR COOKE, EDITOR, BROADCASTER
SMITH COLLEGE, 1954

You may be hitched to one of these creatures we call "Western man" and I think your job is to keep him Western, to keep him truly purposeful, to keep him whole.... This assignment for you, as wives and mothers, has great advantages. In the first place, it is home work—you can do it in the living room with a baby in your lap or in the kitchen with a can opener in your hands.

—ADLAI E. STEVENSON, GOVERNOR, ILLINOIS;
AMBASSADOR TO THE U.N.
SMITH COLLEGE, 1955

I think what surprised me most about the 19th-century writers was their attitude toward women. They assumed with a fine complacency that men were entitled to as much education as they could get but that even a little of it was apt to be dangerous for a woman.

—EDWARD WEEKS, EDITOR, *THE ATLANTIC MONTHLY*
WELLESLEY COLLEGE, 1957

[No one] has gone far enough yet in awakening decision-making people throughout the United States to the significance of women as a manpower resource. Women provide the largest unused, underutilized backlog of brains in the country.

—NEIL MCELROY, SECRETARY OF DEFENSE
WELLESLEY COLLEGE, 1959

Our educated womanpower is our largest single untapped reservoir of talent.

—ABRAHAM RIBICOFF, U.S. REPRESENTATIVE; U.S. SENATOR;
SECRETARY OF HEALTH, EDUCATION, AND WELFARE
MT. HOLYOKE COLLEGE, 1962

Can you have such perpetual insistence upon those aspects of women which are determined by her sex, and not diminish in some degree her other attributes—intellectual power, executive ability, common sense, mature wisdom?... Fifty percent of our brains are locked up on the female side.... Can we afford not to use it in the sciences, in the professions?... Social and individual waste reach a peak when the young woman who has it in her to be, say, a brilliant atomic physicist, or a pioneering sociologist, or an historian of formidable insight finds herself in front of the dishes and the diapers....

Is this, then, the parabola of your future—from scholar to slave?

—ADLAI E. STEVENSON, GOVERNOR, ILLINOIS;
U.N. REPRESENTATIVE
RADCLIFFE COLLEGE, 1963

I don't want to prove the superiority of one sex to another. That would be repeating a male mistake.... What we do know is that the differences between the two sexes ... are much less great than the differences to be found within each group.

—GLORIA STEINEM, WRITER, ACTIVIST
VASSAR COLLEGE, 1970

Women are told today that they can have it all, career, marriage, and children, and I'd like to tell you that if the word "all" means career, marriage, and children, then you can have it....

—BEVERLY SILLS, OPERA SINGER
SMITH COLLEGE, 1985

A woman is a person who makes choices.... A woman is a maker and a molder.... A woman heals others. A woman builds bridges. A woman makes children and makes cars. A woman writes poetry and songs. A woman is a person who makes choices....

What will you choose?

—ELEANOR HOLMES NORTON, ASST. LEGAL DIR., ACLU; EXEC. ASST., MAYOR OF NEW YORK; MEMBER, EEOC WELLESLEY COLLEGE, 1972

Social critic Maria Manis put it best when she wrote, "Nobody objects to a woman being a good writer, or a good sculptor, or geneticist, if at the same time she manages to be a good wife, a mother, good-looking, good-tempered, well dressed, well groomed, and un-aggressive."

—ELIZABETH DOLE, POLITICIAN
WHEATON COLLEGE, 1987

Last night, I dreamt that as I was approaching this podium, I was greeted with a chorus of boos. A young lady came up with a note on which was written, "How dare you accept this invitation to make the commencement address when you are merely holding on to the coattails of the accomplishments of your wife."

—PAUL NEWMAN, ACTOR
SARAH LAWRENCE COLLEGE, 1990

I hope that many of you will run for political office and raise issues of work and family. I particularly hope that more women will run for political office, since we've been struggling to make these balances. We women cannot do a worse job than the men in power so far.

—MARIAN WRIGHT EDELMAN, PRESIDENT,
CHILDREN'S DEFENSE FUND
SOUTHERN METHODIST UNIVERSITY, 1993

ACTIVISM

As you go out today to enter the clamorous highways of life, I should like to discuss with you some aspects of the American dream. For in a real sense, America is essentially a dream, a dream as yet unfulfilled. It is a dream of a land where men of all races, of all nationalities, and of all creeds can live together as brothers. The substance of that dream is expressed in these sublime words, words lifted to cosmic proportions: "We hold these truths to be self-evident, that all men are created equal, and that they are endowed by their Creator with certain inalienable rights; among these rights are life, liberty, and the pursuit of happiness." This is the dream.

One of the first things we notice in this dream is an amazing universalism. It does not say some men, but it says all men. It does not say all white men, but all men, which includes Black men. It does not say all Gentiles, but it says all men, which includes Jews. It does not say all Protestants, but it says all men, which includes Catholics.

—DR. MARTIN LUTHER KING, JR., CIVIL RIGHTS LEADER
LINCOLN UNIVERSITY, PENNSYLVANIA, 1961

Thomas Jefferson spoke of certain truths as self-evident ... he did not say that these truths were self-explanatory or that they were self-operating.

—J. Martin Klotsche, president of the college
Milwaukee State Teachers College, 1952

As a satirist, I can't foresee any administration, Republican or Democratic, under which the basic message of my work wouldn't be the same, that it's possible to do better. This is the true glory of America, this hope is what stirs me as a patriot.

—GARRY TRUDEAU,
CARTOONIST AND CREATOR OF "DOONESBURY"
WAKE FOREST UNIVERSITY, 1986

Some minds are eager for any change, and some are angry at any.

—M. WOOLSEY STRYKER, PRESIDENT OF THE COLLEGE
HAMILTON COLLEGE, 1894

There's no way of eradicating the knowledge of nuclear weapons from the human race. Some way, therefore, must be found to change the attitudes of the people who wish to use them.

—J. WILLIAM FULBRIGHT, FORMER U.S. SENATOR
UNIVERSITY OF MIAMI, 1987

The challenge to all of us ... is to live a revolution, not to die for one. ...

You don't have to play one role in this revolutionary age above all others. If you're willing to pay the price for it, you can do anything you want to do. And the price is worth it.

—GLORIA STEINEM, WRITER, ACTIVIST
VASSAR COLLEGE, 1970

Politicians in administration after administration, heavily influenced by experts treating nuclear devices as simply upgraded conventional weapons, have been convinced that superiority in nuclear weapons is possible. Only rarely and briefly have some realized that all that really counts on either side is sufficiency.

If I have a gun at your forehead, and you have a gun at mine, it makes little difference how many or what kind of guns either you or I have in reserve.

—THOMAS J. WATSON, JR., CHAIRMAN EMERITUS, IBM;
FORMER U.S. AMBASSADOR TO THE USSR
ST. MICHAEL'S COLLEGE, 1982

You are leaders. You are bound to be leaders because you have had advantages that make you leaders to someone, whether you know it or not. There will be tough problems to solve. You have heard about them. You can't solve them with long faces—they don't solve problems, not when they deal with humans. Humans have to have confidence. You have got to help give it to them.

—DWIGHT D. EISENHOWER, U.S. PRESIDENT
DARTMOUTH COLLEGE, 1953

Your challenge is to be our conscience, to keep the drumbeat of activism alive, to rouse those who have become too comfortable for the struggle, and to reinvigorate those too tired to fight.

—RON BROWN, SECRETARY OF COMMERCE
HOWARD UNIVERSITY, 1993

America is still very much a work in progress, and one of the things that most distinguishes it from most other countries is that we have never been afraid to challenge our most cherished assumptions, to ask the impertinent question. We have always been willing to reinvent ourselves for the common good. This is the true glory of your country.

—GARRY TRUDEAU, CARTOONIST AND CREATOR OF "DOONESBURY"
  JOHNS HOPKINS UNIVERSITY, 1990

We are all political actors, aren't we, to be judged by our sins of omission as well as by commission, by our silence as much by our expressed opinions, by what we let slide as much by the things we stand up for.

—MERYL STREEP, ACTRESS
VASSAR COLLEGE, 1985

If your community gives up or fails in its functions the state will surely move in, and your influence is smaller in the state than in your town. . . . If the state fails the Federal government moves in, and your influence is still smaller there.

—CLEO F. CRAIG, PRESIDENT, AT&T
UNIVERSITY OF MISSOURI, 1952

Whenever men have tried to shift their responsibility to government, they have invariably lost the right of individual choice.

—JAMES J. NANCE, PRESIDENT, PACKARD MOTOR COMPANY
OHIO WESLEYAN UNIVERSITY, 1952

We must insist upon the right not to be unified; upon the right not to be integrated; upon the right to an independent viewpoint which is not totally furnished by any single organization.

—CLARK KERR, PROFESSOR, UNIVERSITY OF CALIFORNIA
SWARTHMORE COLLEGE, 1952

Your nation and your state were not created by tired, frightened people, preoccupied with the "good old days" of the past.

—FRANKLIN MURPHY, CHANCELLOR OF THE UNIVERSITY
UNIVERSITY OF KANSAS, 1952

What will it be like to live in a world where the solutions of serious learned people to practically every big problem is not to kill somebody?

—TONI MORRISON, WRITER
SARAH LAWRENCE COLLEGE,
1988

There are always a lot of people so afraid of rocking the boat that they stop rowing. We can never get ahead that way.

—HARRY S. TRUMAN, U.S. PRESIDENT
HOWARD UNIVERSITY, 1952

You have the most serious charge to make this country more than it is today, which is really what we're all about. More than it is today—what James Baldwin called, "these yet to be United States."

—MAYA ANGELOU, POET
SPELMAN COLLEGE, 1983

The nuclear freeze and Central America are only the latest examples of where each of us can make a difference and all of us must try. To put it starkly, we must be involved with the issues or we may become involved in the war.

—EDWARD KENNEDY, SENATOR
TUFTS UNIVERSITY, 1983

Today it is true that all can ride at the front of the bus, but that's not enough. We must have a fair chance to drive that bus, we must have a fair chance to own that bus, and we must have a fair chance to own the bus company.

—WALTER MONDALE, FORMER U.S. VICE PRESIDENT
CLARK COLLEGE, 1983

You will get what you deserve and you will deserve what you get if you do not participate and move out and try to bring about an amelioration of the human condition in this country.

—SHIRLEY CHISHOLM, CONGRESSPERSON
HOWARD UNIVERSITY, 1983

There is no morality in the mushroom cloud.

—EDWARD KENNEDY, SENATOR
BROWN UNIVERSITY, 1983

TRAGICALLY HIP

"These are days you'll remember." If you recall nothing else from your graduation ceremony, remember you heard the New Jersey Governor quote from The 10,000 Maniacs.

> —CHRISTINE TODD WHITMAN, GOVERNOR OF NEW JERSEY
> WHEATON COLLEGE, 1995

Seize the day, seize the future. Use your consciousness. Or, borrowing from Jefferson Starship, "Feed your head." But once you seize the day, and seize the future, what will you do with it?

> —JAY H. BOYLAN, CHAIR OF THE UNIVERSITY FACULTY
> CHAPMAN UNIVERSITY, 1994

To paraphrase the song produced by an inspirational group of artists, you are the world, you are the ones that can make a brighter day.

—GERALDINE FERRARO, POLITICIAN
HUNTER COLLEGE, 1985

As Elvis Costello once said—I surprised you, didn't I?—"Welcome to the working week, I know it don't thrill you I hope it won't kill you."

—ROSE BIRD, CHIEF JUSTICE, CALIFORNIA
HASTINGS COLLEGE, 1986

I'm not a speaker, I'm a performer. If it's all right, could I sing instead? [Sung to the tune of "Louie Louie"] "Come on, it's party time at NYU! Now you get a chance to fly away! But don't forget your alma mater and come back someday! Louie Louie, oh yeah, we gotta go right now, let me hear it, oh Louie Louie."

—NEIL DIAMOND, SINGER
NEW YORK UNIVERSITY, 1995

RELATIONSHIPS

I'm Jerry. Graduation is a time for words of wisdom, thought-provoking words, challenging words, and that is why we have Ben with us today. I will be speaking to you about how we reached our august positions as true ice cream magnates.

Ben and I are old friends from junior high school. We met at Merrick Avenue Junior High School in the seventh grade when we were the two slowest, fattest kids running around the track together. And Coach Phelps was yelling at us, "Gentlemen, you've got to run the mile in under seven minutes. If you don't run the mile in under seven minutes, you're going to have to do it again." And there were Ben and I in this little pack way behind the rest of the pack, and Ben yelled back, "Gee, Coach, if I don't run it in under seven minutes the first time, I'm certainly not going to run it in under seven minutes the second time." And that was when I realized that Ben was someone I wanted to get to know.

—JERRY GREENFIELD
(SPEAKING WITH HIS PARTNER IN BEN & JERRY'S, BEN COHEN)
LONG ISLAND UNIVERSITY, 1995

What role will love play in your life?... Love should be the center of life, the enduring, glowing fire. And I'm happy to see no evidence currently of it dying out. If you don't accept that, I would like to present as evidence Exhibit A over here in the business section. I would like to ask James Vanke and Suzanne Woloski to please stand up. Right here, in the front.

O.K., everybody, James and Suzanne have been dating for over a year and as you can see, they are head over heels in love. And so, folks, right here, in front of thirty thousand people, we are about to witness a big moment. Suzanne didn't know about this. Suzanne, James wants to know if you will do him the honor of becoming his wife.... She said yes. Love conquers all. You're all invited to the wedding.

—DR. FRANCIS S. COLLINS, DIRECTOR,
NATIONAL CENTER FOR HUMAN GENOME RESEARCH
UNIVERSITY OF NORTH CAROLINA AT CHAPEL HILL, 1994

Think of the children first.... We human beings all want to know that we are acceptable.... We need to know we are worth being proud of. I'm proud of you....

Take a minute of silence to think of the people who have loved us along the way, who have helped us become the people that we are.... I wish you a life full of opportunities to help others ... and opportunities to become the best of what you are.

It's such a good feeling to know that you are alive.

—FRED ROGERS ("MISTER ROGERS"), TELEVISION HOST
GOUCHER COLLEGE, 1993

At the level of our daily lives, one man or woman meeting with another man or woman is finally the central arena of history.

—ATHOL FUGARD, PLAYWRIGHT
GEORGETOWN UNIVERSITY, 1984

Assumptions are the termites of relationships.

—HENRY WINKLER, ACTOR
EMERSON COLLEGE, 1995

Do not imagine that personal relationships will run themselves. Like jobs, they are valuable in proportion to the amount of effort they demand. It is a great deal easier to make ten thousand dollars than to run a real marriage or friendship.

—W. H. AUDEN, POET
SMITH COLLEGE, 1940

At my graduation, I thought we had to marry what we wished to become. Now you are becoming the men you once would have wanted to marry.

...We're halfway there. We've begun to raise our daughters more like sons—so now, women are whole people. But fewer of us have the courage to raise our sons more like daughters. Yet until men raise children as much as women do—and are raised to raise children, whether or not they become fathers—they will have a far harder time developing in themselves those human qualities that are wrongly called "feminine," but are really those necessary to raise children: empathy, flexibility, patience, compassion, and the ability to let go.

—GLORIA STEINEM, WRITER, ACTIVIST
SMITH COLLEGE, 1995

At the end of your life you will never regret not having passed one more test, winning one more verdict, or not closing one more deal. You will regret time not spent with a husband, a child, a friend, or a parent.

—BARBARA BUSH, FIRST LADY
WELLESLEY COLLEGE, 1990

Instead of families looking like the Cleavers on *Leave It to Beaver*, we have families that include test-tube babies and surrogate moms. But remember as you go forth, no matter what a family looks like today, the family remains the essential ingredient in shaping our lives, and you have no greater responsibility ahead of you.

—HILLARY RODHAM CLINTON, FIRST LADY
GEORGE WASHINGTON UNIVERSITY, 1994

What matters is how you choose to love. As you know, there's a lot of emphasis placed on success, and I hear it all the time. But what I know is there is no success where there is no joy, so instead of looking for success in your life, look for the thing that is going to bring you the greatest joy. Joy is the only goal really worth seeking.

—OPRAH WINFREY, TELEVISION HOST
SPELMAN COLLEGE, 1993

Make love! Propagate!

—BURGESS MEREDITH, ACTOR
MIDDLEBURY COLLEGE, 1984

REAL HISTORY

The grand affair of launching into the world, takes place in a period of life the most eventful that we ever experience. The wisdom of the serpent is as necessary as the innocence of the dove; and unless our minds are rightly attempered with both, we shall split upon the dangerous shoals before we spy them.

—TIMOTHY DWIGHT, PRESIDENT OF THE COLLEGE
YALE COLLEGE, 1772

The period, in which your lot is cast, is possibly the happiest in the roll of time. It is true, you will scarcely live to enjoy the summit of American glory; but you now see the foundations of that glory laid. A scene like this is not unfolded in an instant. Innumerable are the events in the great system of Providence, which must advance the mighty design before it can be completed. Innumerable must be the actors in so vast a plot, and infinitely various the parts they act. Every event is necessary in the great system, and every character on the extended stage. Some part or other must belong to you, perhaps a capital one. You should by no means consider yourself as members of a small neighborhood, town, or colony only, but as being concerned in laying the foundations of American greatness. Your wishes, your designs, your labors are not to be confined by the narrow bound of the present age, but are to comprehend succeeding generations, and be pointed to immortality.... You may, especially at the present period, be called into the active scenes of a military life. Should this be your honorable lot, I can say nothing, which ought more to influence you, than that you fight for the property, the freedom, the life, the glory, the religion of the inhabitants of this mighty empire; for the cause, for the honor, of mankind and your Maker.

—TIMOTHY DWIGHT, PRESIDENT OF THE COLLEGE
    YALE COLLEGE, 1776

The current fear is not just another war movie, the current fear does not end in two hours and fifteen minutes, but it goes on around the clock, around the world.

—DITH PRAN, CAMBODIAN REFUGEE, NEWS PHOTOGRAPHER
    FAIRFIELD UNIVERSITY, 1986

Justice condemns, even benevolence and charity abhor those men, who trade in human flesh, whose souls are blacker, than the faces of their slaves. There are facts in store, which would chill our souls with horror; which would extinguish the stars; which would blacken the face of darkness; which make Satan envy the superior guilt of man.

—LEONARD WOODS, VALEDICTORIAN
HARVARD COLLEGE, 1796

The relation subsisting between the white and black people of this country is the vital question of the age. ... Here, a man must be hot, or be accounted cold, or perchance, something worse than hot or cold. The lukewarm and the cowardly will be rejected by earnest men on either side of the controversy. The man who avoids it, to gain favor of both parties, will be rewarded with scorn; and the timid man who shrinks from it, for fear of offending either party, will be despised. To the lawyer, the preacher, the politician, and to the man of letters, there is no neutral ground. He that is not for us, is against us.

—FREDERICK DOUGLASS, ABOLITIONIST
WESTERN RESERVE COLLEGE, OHIO,
1854

When the black man shall be permitted to go where he pleases, to earn his own honest living in his own way, to enjoy all the natural rights of a man, and such civil rights as he is fitted for, the country will be quiet. ... We are not to narrow ourselves by prejudice, and fear that the heavens will fall, if we apply impartially and fully those great principles of natural right which are surely from God, and which we have avowed before the world.

—MARK HOPKINS, PRESIDENT OF THE COLLEGE
WILLIAMS COLLEGE, 1863

We of the younger generation especially must feel a sacred call to that which lies before us. I go out to do my little part in helping my untutored brother. We of this less favored race realize that our future lies chiefly in our own hands. On ourselves alone will depend the preservation of our liberties and the transmission of them in their integrity to those who will come after us. And we are struggling on, attempting to show that knowledge can be obtained under difficulties, that poverty may give place to affluence; that obscurity is not an absolute bar to distinction, and that a way is open to welfare and happiness to all who will follow the way with resolution and wisdom, that neither the old-time slavery, nor continued prejudice need extinguish self-respect, crush manly ambition or paralyze effort; that no power outside of himself can prevent man from sustaining an honorable character and a useful relation to his day and generation. We know that neither institutions nor friends can make a race stand unless it has strength on its own foundation; that races like individuals must stand or fall by their own merit, that to fully succeed they must practice their virtues of self-reliance, self-respect, industry, perseverance, and economy.

—PAUL ROBESON, VALEDICTORIAN
RUTGERS UNIVERSITY, 1919

Should someone ask me whether I would indicate the west, such as it is today, as a model today to my country, frankly I would have to answer, No. I could not recommend your society, in its present state, as an ideal for ours. Through intense spiritual suffering our country has now just achieved a spiritual development of such intensity that the western system in its present state of spiritual exhaustion just does not look attractive.

—ALEXANDER SOLZHENITSYN, SOVIET AUTHOR AND DISSIDENT
HARVARD UNIVERSITY, 1978

On this tenth day of June, 1940, the hand that held the dagger has struck it into the back of its neighbor. ... In our American unity, we will pursue two obvious and simultaneous causes: we will extend to the opponents of force the material resources of this nation, and at the same time we will harness and speed up the use of those resources in order that we ourselves in the Americas may have the equipment and training equal to the task of any emergency and every defense. ...

—FRANKLIN D. ROOSEVELT, U.S. PRESIDENT
UNIVERSITY OF VIRGINIA, 1940

(Roosevelt's remarks referred to Italy joining World War II against France and Great Britain. His support of the Allies despite American concerns about sending troops overseas was more pointed because his son, Franklin, Jr., was in the graduating class.)

On this quiet June morning the war is the dreadful background of the thoughts of us all, and it is difficult indeed to think of anything except the agony and death going on a few thousand miles to the east and west of this hall....

It is tempting in this terrible crisis, which may quite conceivably end in temporary disaster, to believe that it is due to the sudden appearance of some unusually wicked men. This is too simple. Man is lazy, impatient, and wicked at all times. Society has come to grief when its members are confronted by problems for which their technique or their metaphysics, or both, are inadequate. Our age is unique, in that for the first time in history men have the technique to create that economy of abundance which can make an open society physically possible. If we fail to overcome our natural weakness, our failure will be a metaphysical failure.

—W. H. Auden, poet
Smith College, 1940

From Stettin in the Baltic to Trieste in the Adriatic, an iron curtain has descended across the Continent.

—WINSTON CHURCHILL, PRIME MINISTER OF GREAT BRITAIN
WESTMINSTER COLLEGE, MISSOURI, 1946

(The expression "iron curtain" had been coined as early as 1920, but had never been used openly by a world leader. Churchill deliberately used the phrase to publicly mark the change in official policy from an alliance with the Soviet Union to the antagonistic Cold War.)

We were a people who turned our back upon Europe and its quarrels. Nearly thirty years ago we fought a war in Europe. It was primarily an effort to secure a Europe that wouldn't bother us. We failed. Now another bitter war has ended. Europe is exhausted.... This country has become the world's banker, and the principal source of food in a world that is hungry.... America is fat; and the rest of the world is lean.... There is real danger that we in America are moving in one direction and the rest of the world is moving in another. There is real and urgent danger that we shall be isolated.... we are in danger of becoming a great straggling island off the coast of Kamchatka with most of the world united against us.

—EDWARD R. MURROW, JOURNALIST
SMITH COLLEGE, 1947

Our policy is directed not against any country or doctrine but against hunger, poverty, desperation, and chaos.

—Gen. George C. Marshall, White House Chief of Staff, announcing the Marshall Plan of relief for Europe (Winston Churchill called it "the most unsordid act in history.")
Harvard University, 1947

The famed "torch" my generation gives you this day is radio-active. . . .

—Philip Wylie, writer
University of Miami, 1952

I love and admire 100% Americans, but I believe that 200% Americans can do as much harm to our free society as can the 0% American.

> —J. C. WARNER, PRESIDENT,
> CARNEGIE INSTITUTE OF TECHNOLOGY
> MT. LEBANON HIGH SCHOOL, 1952

Don't join the book burners. Don't think you are going to conceal faults by concealing evidence that they ever existed. Don't be afraid to go in your library and read every book, as long as that document does not offend our own ideas of decency. That should be the only censorship.

How will we defeat communism unless we know what it is, and what it teaches, and why does it have such an appeal for men, why are so many people swearing allegiance to it? It is almost a religion, albeit one of the nether regions.

And we have got to fight it with something better, not try to conceal the thinking of our own people. They are part of America. And even if they think ideas that are contrary to ours, their right to say them, their right to record them, and their right to have them at places where they are accessible to others is unquestioned, or it isn't America.

—DWIGHT D. EISENHOWER, U.S. PRESIDENT
DARTMOUTH COLLEGE, 1953

The practical aspect of nonviolent resistance is that it somehow exposes the moral defenses of the opponent. Not only that, it somehow arouses his conscience at the same time, and it breaks down his morale. He has no answer for it. If he puts you in jail, that's all right; if he lets you out, that's all right, too. If he beats you, you accept that; if he doesn't beat you—fine. And so you go on, leaving him with no answer. But if you use violence, he does have an answer. He has the state militia; he has police brutality.

... The choice is no longer between violence and nonviolence; it is either nonviolence or nonexistence.

—DR. MARTIN LUTHER KING, JR., CIVIL RIGHTS LEADER
LINCOLN UNIVERSITY, 1961

I speak to you tonight in a spirit of hope. Eighteen years ago the advent of nuclear weapons changed the course of the world as well as the war. Since that time, all mankind has been struggling to escape from the darkening prospect of mass destruction on earth. In these years, the United States and the Soviet Union have frequently communicated suspicion and warnings to each other, but very rarely hope. Our representatives have met at the summit and at the brink; they have met in Washington and in Moscow; in Geneva and at the United Nations. But too often these meetings have produced only darkness, discord, or disillusion.

Yesterday a shaft of light cut into the darkness. Negotiations were concluded in Moscow on a treaty to halt all nuclear tests in the atmosphere, in outer space, and under water. For the first time, an agreement has been reached on bringing the forces of nuclear destruction under international control.

—JOHN F. KENNEDY, U.S. PRESIDENT
AMERICAN UNIVERSITY, 1963

Your imagination, your initiative, and your indignation will determine whether we build a society where progress is the servant of our needs, or a society where old values and new visions are buried under unbridled growth. For in your time we have the opportunity to move not only toward the rich society and the powerful society, but upward to the Great Society.... We have the power to shape the civilization that we want. But we need your will, your labor, your hearts, if we are to build that kind of society.

—LYNDON B. JOHNSON, U.S. PRESIDENT
UNIVERSITY OF MICHIGAN, 1964

What we are engaged in, in Vietnam, is essentially an effort against history. . . .

One can no more reject the past than reject one's own skeleton. . . . In the present time of uncertainty and confusion of values, it is a comfort to know that man has experienced and come through such trials before, several times over.

—BARBARA TUCHMAN, HISTORIAN
RADCLIFFE COLLEGE, 1967

EXIT
LAUGHING

You're college graduates now, so use your education. Remember: It's not who you know, it's whom.

—Joan Rivers, comedian
University of Pennsylvania, 1989

Now, I know there are certain clichés and things that go with commencements, such as the graduation speaker is supposed to tell you that you know more today than you've ever known before than you will never know again. I won't say that.

—Ronald Reagan, U.S. President
Seton Hall University, 1983

Many good things have been said today. I must say you don't get this kind of wisdom from graduating speakers at the Harvard Law School.

—RALPH NADER, ACTIVIST
UNIVERSITY OF CALIFORNIA LAW SCHOOL, 1982

After all of these years of exams and all of these years of studying and working and struggling, and wondering, how are you going to pay back the loans, you deserve to party, for at least a week.

—OPRAH WINFREY, TELEVISION HOST
MEHARRY MEDICAL COLLEGE, 1987

For those of us floundering out here in the real world, to those of you preparing to enter it, may I just say, welcome—we need you.

—GARRY TRUDEAU, CARTOONIST AND CREATOR OF "DOONESBURY"
JOHNS HOPKINS UNIVERSITY, 1990

Commencement means to go forth. *Forth* is not *home.*

—BILL COSBY, COMEDIAN
BROWN UNIVERSITY, 1985

You are no longer tadpoles. The time has come for you to leave the swamp. But I am sure that wherever I go as I travel around the world, I will find each and every one of you working your tails off to save other swamps and give those of us who live there a chance to survive.

... May success and a smile always be yours, even when you are knee-deep in the sticky mud of life.

... All of us should feel very proud of ourselves—and just a little bit silly.

—KERMIT THE FROG,
RECEIVING A "DOCTORATE OF AMPHIBIOUS LETTERS"
LONG ISLAND UNIVERSITY (SOUTHHAMPTON CAMPUS), 1996

[Samantha Chie, a marine biology major, was not amused. She told *The New York Times*, "I've been laboring for five years, and now we have a sock talking at our commencement."]

SOURCES

Newspapers, periodicals, and television news reports:

ABC News

Associated Press

Atlanta Constitution

CBS News

Charlotte Observer

Christian Science Monitor

Detroit Free Press

Entertainment Weekly

Harper's magazine

Houston Post

Knight-Ridder News Service

Los Angeles Times

NBC News

New York Newsday

The New York Times

Newsweek

People

San Francisco Chronicle

San Jose Mercury News

Science

Time

United Press International

U.S. News & World Report

The Washington Post

BIBLIOGRAPHY

Gray, Glenda Ruth, "Women's Proper Place," University of Oregon doctoral dissertation (Ann Arbor, MI: University Microfilms International, 1981).

Horn, Francis H., editor, *Go Forth, Be Strong* (Carbondale: Southern Illinois University Press, 1978).

Podell, Janet and Steven Anzovin, editors, *Speeches of the American Presidents* (New York: H.W. Wilson Co., 1988).